DECEMBER 2021 (PART-2)

AN ANTHOLOGY OF ARTICLES

BRAIN BOOSTER ARTICLES

Contents

Preface

"Start writing, no matter what. The water does not flow until the faucet is turned on".

-Louis L'Amour

Hundreds of students and professors are contributing their work to Brain Booster Articles, we are here to provide ample information about Law and Contemporary issues. Our aim is to provide a platform for today's generation to express their views and ideas on law and contemporary law.

DECORUM AND DRESS CODE IN INDIAN COURTROOMS

Author: Gauri Sharma, IV year of B.B.A.,LL.B. from Symbiosis Law School, Hyderabad

The concept of courtroom decorum is not only a necessity to establish respect for the Judges and the lawyers but an essential measure to render the administration of justice in society. Thus, advocacy is considered a noble profession that cannot be compared with other professions such as business and trade. Professional ethics under the law is generally considered as the duties that are performed by the advocates. Thus, the objective of professional ethics in the legal world is to maintain dignity, decorum and a friendly atmosphere in the work environment that leads to the smooth functioning of the courts.

Decorum Required in the Courtroom

The Bar Council of India has set professional standards for the advocates to be followed in the form of duties which shall be performed towards the courts, their clients, opponents and fellow members which is quite a formal process. Thus, in the courts, the advocates are requested to act in a distinguished manner as while presenting the case before the court, the advocate shall act in a dignified manner and hold him with self-respect. However, in the cases of serious complaints against any judicial officer of the court, the advocate shall have the right to complain and submit grievances to the respected authorities. An advocate shall respect the court and shall bow before the judges as soon as he enters the courtroom. He should keep in mind the dignity and respect for the judicial officers which is essential for the survival of the free community. Moreover, while leaving the courtroom, one shall never show its back to the Judges. An advocate shall not communicate in private as he is barred to communicate to any judge privately.

It is also the duty of the advocate not to act improperly with the opposite counsel, the parties to the case and also prevent his clients to do the same. He shall not refuse to engage with those clients who indulge in illegal activities. Thus, the advocates shall not trust their clients blindly and shall speak in a dignified manner during the arguments presented before the court and shall not damage the reputation of the opposite parties on false grounds. Moreover, an advocate shall not appear before the court or practice for those who are about him such as a father, son, daughter, etc. Such as in Stayendra Singh v. Ram Singh & Ors., the court held that an advocate shall not appear before the court as his wife was a Judge in that case, if he appears, it shall be considered as professional misconduct.[1] The other instances include carrying of firearms in the court proceedings, which shall be also treated against the dignity of the legal profession.[2] An advocate shall not appear for the cases before the court where he is a member or under the management of an establishment until and unless he is appearing as amicus curaie or without any fee for Bar Council or Association or any Incorporated Law Society. Moreover, he shall not appear in the case in which he has a pecuniary interest such as in the bankruptcy petition. In cases of surety or case to certify the soundness of surety for the utility of any legal proceeding, the advocate shall be barred to appear.[3]

The advocate shall wear the prescribed dress code as per the Bar Council of India rules. For instance, the advocates are not allowed to wear their gowns or white bands in public places. Moreover, the advocates have a duty towards their clients such as not to withdraw from service or give full disclosure to clients, etc whereas, under duties towards their fellow members, it includes the duty of not to advertise or promote any unauthorized practices, etc. The other major duties of the advocate that helps in maintaining orderliness in the courtroom include being cooperative with the bench or a judge during proceedings. Also, he shall not laugh or talk loudly in the courtroom especially where the proceedings are going on. He is required to either switch off his mobile phone or put it on silent mode and shall stand on the arrival of the entry of the Judges to mark respect and honour. If an advocate has accepted a case brief, he must attend and be present at all the adjournments and if he has his case in another court during that time, the advocate is obligated to take permission from the respected court. Last but not the least, an advocate cannot leave the court while his proceeding is going on or he shall ensure that his colleagues or juniors take charge of it.[4]

Evolution of Legal Dress Code and Conduct

Every profession consists of a set of rules and guidelines which shall be followed by individuals concerning the dress code or the code of conduct during the period of practice. Such rules of mannerism and decorum are framed to ensure respect for authorities and dignity. In the legal profession, the decorum and the dress code is governed by the Bar Council of India Rules present under the Advocates Act, 1961 which makes it mandatory for every lawyer to wear a black robe with a white shirt followed by a white neckband which not only increases the confidence among lawyers but also act as a measure to ensure discipline in such profession.[5]

The evolution of dress codes begins from the era of the middle ages where the lawyers also called solicitors, barristers used to dress like judges such as in Britain, barristers used to wear a black gown, coifs, skullcaps with long gloves based on the rules of Inns of Court which was the supervisor of education and governed membership of the barristers. However, the barrister who didn't have any case before the court, used to wear open gowns with winged sleeves.[6] However, in the 17th century, the dress code was decided based on taste and preferences based on seasons such as in winter, to keep judges warm, violet silk gowns were worn by the judges and replaced by miniver in summer. Coming into the 21st century, the dress code faced a huge transformation concerning the colours and authorities deciding for the same. In this period, the barristers in Britain used to wear black silk gowns over the suits with a tie, wig and bands.

The black colour represents to depict submission to God and in the case of the legal profession; it symbolizes submission to Justice. Thus, the black gown provides a sense of seriousness, uniqueness and conveys knowledge, authority and steadiness of such individuals whereas white represents light and goodness which also portrays that law is blind.[7]

Regulations of Dress Code in India

"Part VI- Chapter IV, The Regulations of the Bar Council of India Dress Code under Sec. 49(1) (gg) of the Advocates Act, 1961" prescribes the dress code of the advocates in Indian Courtroom which contains the form of dress/robes that shall be worn by advocates considering various factors such as weather conditions occurring before any tribunal or a court. Thus, the dress code includes a coat which shall be black in colour and buttoned up or the other alternatives include black sherwani, achkan, chapkan worn with a white band followed by the gown or it can be a black open breast coat as well followed by a white-collar which may be stiff or soft with a white band and the gown. In both, cases, long trousers of colours such as white, black, grey or dhoti shall be allowed excluding the jeans. Also, a black-tie shall be worn in any other courts except the courts such as Supreme Court, High Courts, District, Sessions and City Civil Courts as in such courts, the white bands shall be worn. The white band consisting of two pieces depicts innocence which together is known as "Tablets of Law laws or Tablets of Stones" as according to Christian belief, these tablets were used by Moses for carving commandments from a burning bush, the white band is considered to have a similar shape to that of tablets which symbolizes the upholding of laws created by God and Men.

For women, the same guidelines have been given. In addition to that, women may wear a black full-sleeved jacket or a blouse with a band. Also, they may wear a saree, long skirts or flares which may be black and white in colour or grey or striped. The options include a Punjabi dress which salwar suit with or without a dupatta. Moreover, the advocate's gown is kept as non-compulsory instead in SC or HC.

Considering the attire of senior advocates in India, the Advocates Act does not specify any regulations for the same but Senior Advocates wear a divergent gown consisting of a Queen's Counsel gown. On the other hand, the dress code of Judges is similar to that of Senior Advocates. Thus, the judges wear a white shirt with trousers followed by a white band and a black gown whereas female judges have also an option of traditional wear. According to the rules, he shall not be allowed to wear a band or a gown at general gatherings. Thus, restricting their use only to the courts or allowing at such events where the Bar Council permits and any violation of such rule may result in professional misconduct. Due, to COVID- 19, since virtual hearings are prevalent, the Supreme Court has directed the advocates to wear plain white shirts/ kurta with the neckband. Moreover, the High Courts have also notified a change in such dress code until further orders based on the medical exigencies. However, public interest litigation has been filed in Allahabad High Court for a ban on the existing dress code of lawyers where the notice has been issued to BCI as well as the Centre recently as the present dress code is not suitable according to the climatic conditions and it violates Articles 14, 21 and 25 of the Indian Constitution.[8]

<u>Conclusion</u>

From the present research, it can be concluded that the duties of an advocate are wide where the main duty of an advocate is to maintain the decorum of court and act nicely towards the colleagues, opponents and other staff which shall be performed with due diligence. He shall always work for the interest of his clients and shall keep the information between them confidential. Advocates are the officers of the court and prestigious members of the community. Thus, they should act fearlessly while keeping their points in court. As studied, the Bar Council of India prohibits activities such as having private communication with the judges for pending cases, such types rules and regulation not only helps the litigants and the parties to the case but also help to sustain the faith and inspiration in the eyes of the general public. It has also been observed the dress code followed in Indian courts is a matter of seriousness which ensures pride and discipline in the legal profession and any violation of it can result in serious repercussions such as during online hearing of a bail application, the High Court of Gujarat fined an advocate a penalty of Rs, 10,000 for just wearing a vest during the proceedings. And various other instances have been witnessed by the Judges across the country.[9] Therefore, all the duties under the Advocates Act for morals and ethics helps to ensure earnestness in the legal profession and makes one be at a superior and reach to a successful level of position

[1] Stayendra Singh v. Ram Singh & Ors.,AIR 1984 SC 1755.

[2] UP Sales Tax Service Association v. Taxation Bar Association, AIR 1996 SC 98.

[3] BCI, Rules of Professional Standards, (October, 7,2021, 4:12 PM), http://www.barcouncilofindia.org/about/professional-standards/rules-on-professional-standards/

[4] Niharika, Advocate's Duty towards the Court, (October, 8, 2021, 5:30 PM), https://www.legalserviceindia.com/legal/article-2373-advocate-s-duty-towards-court.html .

[5] Lynda K Hopewell, Appropriate Attire and Conduct for an Attorney in Courtroom (7 October, 2021, 122:!5 PM), https://www.law.ua.edu/pubs/jlp_files/issues_files/vol12/vol12art13.pdf

[6] Shaheen Parween, Lawyer's Dress Code: Evolution and Practice, (7October, 2021,4:16 PM), https://www.indialegallive.com/special-story/lawyers-dress-code-evolution-practice/

[7]Janet Reno, Historical Background in Wearing Black Robes by Advocates, (October 7,2021, 10:55 PM),

https://www.legalserviceindia.com/legal/article-665-historical-background-in-wearing-black-robes-by-advocates.html

[8] Re Ashok Pandey, Suo Moto Contempt Petition No. 1493 of 2021.

[9] Hindustan Times, Judges shocked as advocate appears shitless, (October 7, 2021, 6:12 PM), https://www.hindustantimes.com/india-news/this-is-something-unpardonable-judges-shocked-as-advocate-appearsshirtless-for-online-hearing/story-g9rLVictYmQHOmWG2KOu5L.html .

CHAPTER TWO

A COMPARATIVE STUDY OF EXECUTIVE REMUNERATION IN INDIA AND THE UNITED KINGDOM

Author: Jeffy Johnson, I year of LLM Corporate and Commercial Law from School of Law, CHRIST (Deemed to be University)

Jeffy Johnson

THE NEW REGIME: 2013 ACT

Section 198 of the Companies Act down a limit on the remuneration in India it is to be considered an administrative imposition. This helps in controlling unregulated pay or excessive remuneration being granted to directors. It is not arbitrary, but it regulates the usage of corporate power. This, in turn, prevents undue influence on pay and performance. A means of accountability will be developed in companies. Shareholders will have the decision-making power to ensure and look into the welfare and betterment of the company. Other components such as profits, size of the corporates, and so on are ignored in the presence of this standard that states the prescribed ceilings in the overall markets.

An additional check on executive remuneration is provided in Section 200 of the Companies Act. This prevents free of taxes to executives who receive pay from the companies. This facilitates maintaining transparency and a check and balance system on the remuneration scale of the executives. Only public and private, which are subsidiaries of public companies, fall under this purview.

The private companies enjoy the exception to this Section without any inference of statutory ceiling. Shareholders' take and opinion should be exercised reasonably with due diligence on the executive remuneration 1956 Act critiqued for the flaws for not safeguarding the minority shareholders. The deadlocks were expected to be met by the proposed Company Law Bill of 2009[1].

DISCLOSURE REQUIREMENT: SCHEDULE V & COMPANIES ACT, 2013

Schedule V of the SEBI (LODR) Regulations, 2015, deals with all financial transactions that should be disclosed in the annual report of the non-executive directors. It also goes on to lay down the criteria of making payments to non-executive directors as well. It also considers the disclosures concerning remuneration that includes all the elements of the pay package of directors concise under salary, bonuses, stock options, etc.[2], secondly, regarding fixed component and performance-linked incentives. Then Service contracts, notice period, and severance fees. Lastly, details of stock options, if any, in scenarios where they are issued at a discount along with the period over that is accrued and over which is exercisable.

Section 197(16) of the Companies Act 2013 was inserted by The Companies (Amendment) Act, 2017. In his report, it deals with the company's auditor shall as per Section 143. The statement as to whether the company's remuneration is paid to the directors is in line with the provisions of this section. And also in case, the compensation paid to any director is over the limit prescribed in this section to provide information regarding the same.

JUDGMENTS ON EXECUTIVE REMUNERATION

In Swabey v. Port Darwin Gold Mining Co. Ltd 1899., In Swabey Case, in the company's articles, "the directors shall each receive by way of remuneration out of company funds in each year the sum of £200, and the chairman also £100 per annum." It means that a director who makes his resignation from the company during the current year is concluded that the resigned director is provided with an apportioned portion of the remuneration of that year[3].

In many cases, the court went on the erroneous assumption in Swabey v. Port Darwin Gold Mining Co. Ltd. (1899) 1 Meg 385. the articles of the company mentioned that the remuneration has to be paid to the directors "at the rate of £200 per annum," was stated in this judgment. But this was irrelevant. This is because the remuneration clause did not have 'at the rate' words in it. The terms mentioned in the clause were extracted from the registered articles, and the decision in the case was grounded as it lacked accuracy. Thus it needed reconsideration, as highlighted in Inman v. Ackroyd (1901)[4].

In the case of Canara Workshops Ltd. vs. Union of India 1965[5], the legislature intends that the remuneration earned in whatever capacity should be brought within a particular limit, it has been so expressed in clear terms; section 348(1), which pertains to the remuneration of the managing agent, is an example. If the limit of 11 percent. Specified in section 198(1) was intended to cover every kind of remuneration earned in whatever capacity, then there would have been no need to enact the prohibition contained in section 348(1). It is because of the limit of 11 percent. It is confined only to managerial remuneration and does not extend to any other kind of remuneration, that there was the necessity for section 348(1). In my view, the compensation payable to directors under section 309[6] is part of the managerial remuneration dealt with under section 198. The limitations in section 309 do not extend to any other kind of remuneration earned in a capacity different from that of the director.

Executive remuneration is provided in Section 309. The section states that compensation should be paid to the directors. The determination of the compensation can be decided through articles of the company or by passing a resolution in the general meeting[7]. It can be a special or ordinary resolution as provided in the articles of the company.

Ruby Mills Limited And Another vs. Union Of India And Another 1984[8] "Having given our careful thought to this matter, we have concluded that section 198 was intended to apply to remuneration for managerial and, therefore, we have recommended the addition of the word 'managerial' between the words 'total ' and 'remuneration' in sub-section (1)."

Commissioner of Income Tax Vs. Amalgamation Pvt. Ltd 1997[9], the directors of the subsidiary companies entered into a service agreement. These subsidiary companies were not identified as the directors of the assessee company. Section 198 of the Companies Act, 1956 'fixing a ceiling on the overall managerial remuneration at 11% of the company's net profits, it was impossible for the subsidiary companies to pay the contracted remuneration to the persons concerned'. In 1959 the assessee company's board of directors passed a resolution to resolve the remuneration to be paid to the subsidiary company's nine directors will be paid according to the terms contracted by them. And any amount above the maximum amount permissible under the 1956 Act will be fulfilled by the assessee company.

R. Balarami Reddy vs. Sutanu Sinha 2020[10] In the case of R. Balarama Reddy, the main question was permissible under Section 197 of the Companies Act, 2013. In the current situation, the Companies Act, 2013 provides that the company cannot pay remuneration more than the prescribed level. In case any payment is made in excess to managerial persons by the company if need to refund such payments. The claim made in the case was not accepted as there was no central government approval taken.

EXECUTIVE REMUNERATION IN THE UNITED KINGDOM: LAWS AND REGULATIONS

EXISTING UK REGIME

There is no statutory limit or set of prescribed structures available in the United Kingdom for executive remuneration. The companies on the London Stock Exchange's primary market are premium listed companies, and many of the other quoted companies must strictly adhere to the United Kingdom Corporate Governance Code.

This Code provides principles and guidelines on components of the directors' remuneration and its extent. It also makes it a need for companies to comply with it and explains the consequences for non-compliance. These principles provided in the code are backed by the best practice guidelines recommended by investors to the shareholders related to voting on such resolution provided by the companies is published.

Section D of the UK Corporate Governance Code[11] sets out specific remuneration requirements for directors. No restrictive caps should be laid down for the remuneration levels; instead, they should be sufficient to safeguard individual quality. The performance of the individual should be giving a significant proportion of the remuneration. Supporting this Association of British Insurers (ABI) Principles of Executive Remuneration (29 September 2011)[12] made a recommendation that policies relating to remuneration should give prime importance to performance. There should be a promotion of the company's sustainable financial health and effective risk management mechanism.

It should allow executives to have an interest similar to the shareholders and hold a significant stake in the corporate. National Association of Pension Funds (NAPF) 2011 and Corporate Governance Policy and Voting Guidelines (November 2011) laid down specific issues. Specifically, that led to a voting sanction that includes in circumstances of excess inflation base salary increases as well.

Remuneration should be given due consideration by the remuneration committees and what compensation will be expected in the times of early termination. The purpose of this is to avoid poor performance from validation and reward.

The corporates should adopt a transparent method setting up of remuneration policies as well as executive's pay. Pensions Investment Research Consultants says that the divergences present in the current or existing remuneration policy should be scrutinized and approved by the owners of the company the shareholders.

There should be a remuneration committee that the board should set up, and it should consist of non-executive directors who decide the remuneration for top executives. This compensation includes both pension and termination payments. If the chairman wishes to be a committee member, he should be independent on his appointment. Publishing the terms of reference is a mandate by the remuneration committee. The PIRC has made a recommendation that the remuneration committee should consist of an employee representative. This will ensure better decision-making[13].

The executives are not entitled to decide once their remuneration. There can be consultation taken from the chief executive regarding the proposal of compensation by the remuneration committee. This is allowed if the chief executive is the authority responsible for the appointment of any consultants. However, NAPF states that 'remuneration consultants should not be involved in the decision-making process. This is a voluntary code, and it states how a conflict of interest may arise between client companies and remuneration consultants. This can be curbed to a certain extent by integrity, competence, confidentiality, due care, objectivity, and transparency principles[14].

In the United Kingdom, the shareholders are not happy after consulting a remuneration consultant as their advice only leads to executive remuneration upwards. However, these numerous FTSE 100 companies instruct such consultants for no good. NAPF notes 'that shareholders may vote against schemes if there is poor alignment between the incentives and shareholders' interests.

DIRECTOR'S ENTITLEMENT TO REMUNERATION

The case of Hutton V. West Cork Railway Co[15] stated that it could be said as a default that directors have no law that governs the remuneration entitled to them. Unless the contrary is enshrined in the company's Articles of Associations, it can be utilizing a separate service contract or AoA[16]. In the case of Re Lundy Granite Co[17], it was held that The article of association lays down explicit provisions and a decision-making process to ascertain the remuneration of the directors. Suppose there is an appropriate provision for executive pay. In that case, directors will be treated as ordinary creditors of the company during the winding up[18], and remuneration will be payable whether the company makes a profit or not. In Re George Newman and Co[19], the company's directors have no power to pay themselves or others in the company. It requires the approval of the constitution of the company.

The House of Lord's case of Guinness PLC V. Saunders[20] held that according to the articles of association of the company, the payment of the directors is void if not decided by the whole board. In the case of Brown and Green Ltd v Hays[21], where the directors pay the remuneration to themselves from the company's funds, it is not entertaining, and the director is compelled to restore it. However, they thought it is permissible. In the case of Re Richmond Gate Property Co Ltd[22], it was stated that the court in cases where the articles association fails to determine the remuneration, the court has the authority to determine the director's salary.

REMUNERATION DISCLOSURE REQUIREMENTS AND SHAREHOLDERS

It is the sole responsibility of the directors to disclose information concerning executive remuneration. Before CA 2006 in CA 1985[23], the disclosure requirements were of limited nature. According to Section 232, the mere need for the directors to disclose the emoluments of the directors and the chairman's highest payment, all the directors aggregate emoluments and loss of office payments.

The information that failed to provide the highest-paid directors was or on the remuneration of individual directors. The Act did not lay down any mechanism in which the disclosure could be made, and the components of the remuneration package of the highest-paid director were not broken down. The examination of executive remuneration was an arduous task, and also, the shareholders only have access to limited information[24].

The limitation in the CA 1985 paved to the Directors' Remuneration Report Regulations 2002 (DRRR 2002)[25] that put in numerous new provisions into the CA 1985. Later it was transplanted to the CA 2006. The Enterprise and Regulatory Reform Act 2013[26] disclosure requirements were introduced in the CA 2006.

When an efficient framework is created to ensure accountability and transparency, only disclosure requirements can be optimal. If the disclosure requirement provides information regarding executive remuneration, the shareholders will rale the right decision. In scenarios where the shareholders do not approve the remuneration report, the company needs to reconsider the remuneration system.

THE PRINCIPLES OF REMUNERATION FOR 2021

The revised Principles of Remuneration for 2021 was published by the Investment Association (IA). This was done along with the letter to the Remuneration Committee (REMCO) chaired with guidance on the COVID-19 impact. According to the Investment Association, the shareholders will scrutinize the executive remuneration intensely due to the pandemic. It also says that the remuneration committee should exercise reasonableness, be diligent, and not negate the executive or isolate them. As the pandemic has affected the companies, they are against provided remuneration to the executives to reduce pay.

The REMCOs motivate to seek a nexus between incentivizing the management. The reality reflects the shareholders, including the employees and the society that is the stakeholders at large. In scenarios where corporates have raised the capital from government support or shareholders, the Investment association says there is no need for bonus payments to the executives for 2020-2021 unless it is unavoidable.

The changes to the Principles for 2021 introduced are as follows. The shareholding policies Post-employment are REMCOs duty to make sure that they need effective post-employment shareholding policies in situ and state how such policies are being enforced after a director has left the corporate. Then the utilization of non-financial performance measures in variable remuneration, the Investment Association be precautious against the increasing use of strategic and private performance metrics for annual bonuses[27].

Where non-financial measures are used, the IA wants the companies to possess a disclosure requirement to showcase the particular achievement which has led to the payment of those elements. Deferral of bonuses the whole portion of a bonus above 100% of salary must now be deferred into shares. There's also a renewed specialization in the extent of executive pensions, which is discussed within the letter to the Remuneration Committee Chairs.

CONCLUSION AND SUGGESTION

APPROVALS REQUIRED FOR DIRECTORS' REMUNERATION

Concerning the approval needed for the directors' remuneration in India in a listed public company and other specific public companies, it should have a nomination and remuneration committee. The committee must ensure and make suggestions as well as recommend policy concerning the remuneration of the directors. The committee gives these recommendations to the board. The maximum managerial in a public company paid to its directors is 11% of its net profit in any financial year. This threshold prescribed in the Companies Act, 2013 can only exceed if it is permitted and approved by the company's shareholders subject to the provision in the 2013 Act. The managing director, whole-time director, or manager's remuneration should not be more than 5% of its net profit. In scenarios where more than one director is present, the total remuneration should not be more than 10% of the company's net profits. In the case of other directors, it should not be more than 1% paid as remuneration from the net profits if there is a whole-time director or manager or 3% in any other matter. This can occur except with the company's prior approval by passing a special resolution in the general meeting. The board's approval to the executive pay is subject to the resolution passes in the coming general meeting of the company in case it is needed as per the Companies Act, 2013.

In the United Kingdom, the quoted company's directors' remuneration report must be approved by the board of directors. It also requires signing on behalf of the board by the secretary or the director. These quoted companies' directors' remuneration reports should consist of the directors' remuneration policy. This remuneration policy depends on the shareholder's binding vote for a minimum of 3 years the annual report on the remuneration when implemented in the financial year being a report on. As well as how the current policy requires to be implemented in the coming financial year depends on the shareholders' annual advisory vote.

LEVEL OF DISCLOSURE

Concerning depends of Indian companies' disclosure, the annual returns should include the disclosure requirement regarding key managerial personnel and directors. The board report should contain an extract of the annual return of the company. In the list companies, the registrar of the companies and stock exchange file the annual returns.

Whereas in the United Kingdom, the annual accounts of all companies should consist of the directors' benefits and remuneration in detail. According to the Companies Act 2006, the quoted companies should provide a detailed remuneration report every year to their shareholders.

REMUNERATION COMMITTEE

In India, public companies can be listed or unlisted. The remuneration committee should accept the director's remuneration, and it should be within limits specified. The remuneration committee will include a minimum of 3 non-executive independent directions, and this will include a nominee director as well.

Whereas in the United Kingdom, the remuneration committee of quoted companies should consist of 3 members. In this, all must be independent. That is, the chairman should be independent, and the non-executive director should be present. It should execute the task of ascertaining the remuneration for all executives and the chairman. It does not encourage non-executive directors' performance-based remuneration and share option.

EXECUTIVE REMUNERATION: CURRENT TIME COVID 19 SOLUTION TO KEEP UP THE SPACE

Firstly, when it comes to appreciating the executives' actions, there should be a broader approach. It should be done reasonably, and it should encourage both the scrutiny of the shareholders. There should be consistency and fairness employed; favourable reward should be rendered; simultaneously, companies facing difficulty remunerating their executives should have favourable reward interventions and analyse the trends. They should decide on executive remuneration programs in the coming year when the market is analysed. They should always keep in mind the long-term perspective of the programs as the shareholders' expectations. There should be a better retention program, special award schemes to encourage the critical talent of the executives. There is a requirement to modify the pay rates of the jobs as well. The workforce strategy should be upgraded. To conclude, the executive remuneration should agree with the changing times. The Board should have oversight and should ensure the profitability of the company.

SUGGESTIONS AND FINDINGS

The fact that executives are remunerated excessively is due to the notion that this will aid them to perform efficiently towards the betterment of the company and its shareholders. It is to be understood that increasing the remuneration of the executives does not result in a hike in their productivity level. The remuneration Committee should set up more effective performance targets and create a coping mechanism against blind faith in the benchmarking system.

This research showcases that the executives are concerned about their respective roles. The corporate governance is weak, and the board of directors is not bothered about the shareholders' interest. All this does not cause any barrier to the remuneration of the executive. Thus the corporate governance is not good is a huge constraint. There is no accountability from the board to the shareholders. There is a need for reform in corporate governance. This will create a regulatory rein over the remuneration of the executive, but this is possible only through an amendment of the existing policies. Issues such as agency problems, corporate governance structure, and other related components do not allow the board of directors to favor the shareholders. There are many externalities that good corporate governance has to overcame. These externalities do not directly affect the governance decision making, but it does have an adverse effect. In scenarios where the executives are remunerated excessively, it is because there is poor corporate governance. The solution to this is that if the shareholders invest in a sound corporate governance system, the excessive executive remuneration can be regulated and reduced.

[1] CHAPTER XIII.APPOINTMENT AND REMUNERATION OF MANAGERIAL PERSONNEL. Companies Act, 2013 Available at:<https://taxguru.in/company-law/managerial-remuneration-companies-act-2013.html> [Online] [Accessed 4 March 2021]. [2] I. Sridhar. Corporate Governance in Listed Companies in India. Available at:<https://www.coursehero.com/file/16769848/Clause-49-Listing-Agreement-by-ISridhar/> [online] [Accessed 10 March 2021]. [3] (1899) 1 Meg 385 [4] 1 KB 613 [5] 1966 36 CompCas 553 Kar [6] 309. Remuneration of directors. [7] Managerial Remuneration. September, 2020. Available at: <https://cleartax.in/s/managerial-remuneration> [Online] [Accessed 20 March 2021]. [8] (1985) 57 Comp. Cas. 193 (Bom.) [9] AIR 1997 SC 2404 [10] [2020]219CompCas281 [11] Section D: Remuneration Executive directors' remuneration should be designed to promote the company's long-term success. [12] PLC Share Schemes & Incentives. New ABI executive remuneration guidelines: September 2011. [Online] Available at: <https://uk.practicallaw.thomsonreuters.com/ 9-508-6287?transitionType=Default&contextData=(sc.Default)&firstPage=true> [Accessed 4 March 2021]. [13] Available at: < https://www.pirc.co.uk/>[online] [Accessed 3 March 2021] [14] Available at :< https://www.remunerationconsultantsgroup.com/?P=THE_CODE#> [online] [Accessed 3 March 2021] [15] (1883) 23 Ch D 654 [16] Charlotte Villiers, Maria Isabel and Huerta Viesca, 'Controlling Directors' Pay in English Law and Spanish Law' (1995) 2(4) Maastricht J. Eur. & Comp. L. 377, 381. [17] (1872) 26 LT 673 [18] The Insolvency Act 1986, Part 4, Chapter V, s 107. [19] [1895] 1 Ch 674 [20] [1990] 2 AC 663 [21] (1920) 36 TLR 330 [22] [1965] 1 WLR 335 [23] CA 1985. Available at: <https://www.legislation.gov.uk/ukpga/1985/6/contents/ enacted>[Online] [Accessed 8 March 2021] [24] Charlotte Villiers, 'Narrative Reporting and Enlightened Shareholder Value Under the Companies Act 2006' in Keay A and Loughrey J (eds), Directors' Duties and Shareholder Litigation in the Wake of the Financial Crisis (Edward Elgar Publishing 2013) 97. [25] The Directors' Remuneration Report Regulations 2002. Available at: <https://www.legislation.gov.uk/uksi/2002/1986/ contents/made>[online] [Accessed 8 March 2021] [26] Enterprise and Regulatory Reform Act 2013. Available at: <https://www.legislation.gov.uk/ukpga/2013/24/contents/enacted> [online] [Accessed 8 March 2021] [27] Baker McKenzie.United Kingdom: Revised IA Principles of Remuneration for 2021 and updated guidelines

from the ISS. A focus on the impact of the pandemic on executive remuneration. November 26 2020. Available at:< https://www.lexology.com/library/
detail.aspx?g=d594cd47-8de3-4d75-b1f4-a54cfca2a580>[Online] [Online] Accessed [February 24 2021]

CHAPTER THREE

CAPITAL PUNISHMENT IN INDIA

Author: Ankita Kandari, III year of B.A.,LL.B.(Hons.) from Law College Dehradun (Uttaranchal University)

Abstract

A developing country as India is similarly there is an increase in the crime rate also. The number of legislations has been enacted still the crime is increasing. Among the various forms of punishment provided in the Indian constitution one such severe form of punishment that is debatable is capital punishment also known as the Death Penalty. China has the highest number of executions per annum and excluding China, Saudi Arabia, iron and Iraq are the three countries responsible for more than 80% of the execution. 108 countries of the world have retained death punishment and 56 have abolished it. In this article, the basic introduction, evolution theories, Doctrine of Rarest of Rare, constitutional validity, the debate between human rights and capital punishment etc. have been explained.

Keywords: capital punishment, death penalty, crimes, murder, crimes

Introduction

The word capital punishment also called the death penalty finds its origin from the word capital crimes /offences which are those crimes that are punishable by death. Some of the capital offences include murder, mass murder, terrorism, treason, espionage, piracy, drug trafficking, war crimes crimes against humanity, genocide and many more depending on the law of the country. Capital punishment means the legal killing of the wrongdoer by the state as punishment for crime. Etymologically, the term capital punishment is derived from the Latin word 'capitalism' in which lit refers to 'of the head' and caput refer to the head so it means execution by beheading. Death sentence means convicting a person with death and the act of carrying out that sentence is known as an execution.

According to the Bureau of Justice Statistics– Capital Punishment refers to the process of sentencing convicted offenders to death for the most serious crimes and carrying out that sentence. The specific offences and circumstances which determine if a crime is eligible for a death sentence are defined by statute and are prescribed by congress or any state legislature.

Evolution /origin of the death penalty

In the Code of King Hammurabi of Babylon which can be traced back to the Eighteen century, the death penalty was codified for 25 different crimes. The Draconian Code of Athens also made the death penalty compulsory for the commitment of all types of crimes. Before the tenth-century criminals were punished with harsh punishment like burning alive, drowning, cutting off limbs etc. The customary method of execution by hanging became common in Britain after the 10th century. Subsequently, it was not allowed except in cases of war.

Evolution in India

The provision for the death penalty for murder in the Indian Penal Code of 1861 was retained by India at Independence. Despite the idea of abolition of the death penalty during the drafting of the Indian constitution between 1947 and 1949, no such provision was incorporated. Private bills were introduced in both the houses of the parliament but none were adopted successfully. It was estimated that two or three people were hanged annually.

The constitutional validity of the death penalty and doctrine of rarest of rare

The first case dealing with the constitutional validity of the death penalty was Jagmohan Singh v. State of Uttar Pradesh. The appellant held section 302 of IPC as violative of Article 14, article 19 and article 21 of the Indian constitution. But the five-judge bench rejecting the contention held the death penalty to be constitutionally valid. The decision to award the death sentence was made by the compliance of the mandate of Article 21 of the constitution of India. In Rajender Prasad v. State of Uttar Pradesh, it was held that capital punishment would not be justified unless it is shown to the society that the criminal was dangerous to the society. The court held ' if the murderous operation of a diehard criminal jeopardizes social security in a persistent, planned and perilous fashion then his employment of fundamental rights may be rightly annihilated'. The Supreme court in Bachan Singh v. Union of India reiterated the decision made in Maneka

Gandhi v. Union of India and held that the death penalty is an exceptional punishment that must be awarded in the "gravest cases of extreme culpability." Thus the death penalty was restricted to the rarest of rare cases. In addition, there was no violation of the basic character of the constitution by the death penalty for murder offences granted under section 302 of IPC.

In Macchi Singh v State of Punjab, the criteria for assessing whether a crime fell into the category of rarest of rare was laid down. The criteria included –

(i) Manner of the commission of murder–If the commission of the murder took place in a barbaric, devilish or treacherous manner. For instance, if the body of the victim is cut into pieces or when the victim has been subjected to inhumane acts of cruelty.

(ii) Motive of the commission of murder- If the murder shows meanness and total depravity. For instance a cold-blooded murder with the motive of inheriting the property or a murder committed in the course of betrayal of motherhood.

(iii) Socially abhorrent nature of the crime– Act involving the murder of a person belonging to the scheduled caste or minority community which arouses social wrath. Dowry death is also known as bride burning is one such example.

(iv) Magnitude of the crime– Gravity of the crime is one such criterion for deciding. If the crime is enormous in proportion like mass murder like the murder of a whole family or community or locality are committed.

(v) Personality of the victim of murder– If the victim is an innocent child, helpless woman public figure and the murder is committed for political or other similar reasons.

The court in the case of Vatheeswaran v. State of Tamil Nadu has held that the delay in execution of the death penalty is unfair, unreasonable, unjust and inhumane which deprives the convict of the basic human rights under article 21 of the constitution of India.

<u>**Crimes for which the death penalty can be awarded**</u>

(i) Aggravated murder- Section 302 of the Indian Penal code provides the death penalty or (imprisonment for life) as punishment.

(ii) Terrorism related offences not resulting in death- The death penalty is the punishment in case of use of any special category of explosive to cause an explosion that could endanger the life or cause serious property damage.

(iii) Rape not resulting in death–Under the Criminal law Act, 2013 a person who inflicts injury in a sexual assault that results in death or is left in a 'vegetative state' may be punished with death.

(iv) Drug trafficking not resulting in death -A person convicted of a commission or attempt to commit drug trafficking or financing of a certain type of narcotic and psychotropic substances can be sentenced to death.

(v) Treason- Any person who wages or try to wage a war against the nation or government or helps the Navy, Army, Airforce, soldiers or member to commit a mutiny can be convicted for the death sentence.

(vi) Military offences not resulting in death– Mutiny, abetment of assault or attempt to seduce airmen, soldiers and sailors from their duty are punishable by death.

(vii) Other offences resulting in death

- armed robbery
- abduction for money where the victim is killed
- committing or helping others to commit sati

(viii) Other offences not resulting in death

- attempt to kill those sentenced to life imprisonment
- providing false evidence with the intention of conviction of that person

Category of offenders excluded from capital punishment

(i) Minor- the Juvenile Justice Act defines a boy who has not attained the age of 16 years and a girl who has not attained the age of 18 years as a juvenile. Section 22 of the Juvenile Justice Act provides that no delinquent juvenile shall be sentenced to death.

(ii) Pregnant women- Section 416 of the Criminal Procedure Code provide that if a woman who has been sentenced to death is found to be pregnant then the high court shall order the execution of the sentence to be postponed and may if it thinks fit to commute the death sentence to imprisonment for life.

(iii) Intellectually disable-Who is either mentally ill or not able to understand the nature of the act.

Capital punishment and human rights

The use of the death penalty is a matter of huge debate around the world, whether it should exist or not. Protection of life and personal liberty has been provided under Article 21 of the Indian Constitution. There are some inherent rights to which a human being is entitled since birth and the right to life is one such right. Death is a phenomenon of irreversible nature and death often is regarded as the justice of revenge by the statesmen. Countries like the United States, China, Korea, Japan, and Pakistan including India are some countries where the death penalty is awarded as a punishment. China tops as the country where the execution is the highest. The application of the death penalty has always been a matter of debate among lawyers, judges, jurists and administrators. Criminals, like other humans, also deserve some basic human rights but considering the viewpoint of the victims, it is necessary to provide justice to them. The United Nations General Assembly has recognised that those countries that have not abolished the death penalty should administer it only in the rarest of rare cases. The person below the age of 16 years, pregnant women, new mothers and insane persons have been exempted from the punishment. Besides the right of appeal has also been granted to the people. It has been made mandatory that while the appeal is pending the punishment should not be executed.

Law commission report on death penalty 2015

On 31ˢᵗ August 2015, the Law Commission of India chaired by Justice A.P Shah submitted its 262ⁿᵈ report. In Santosh Kumar, Satish Bhushan Bariyar v. Maharashtra and Shankar Kisanrao Khade v. Maharashtra the Supreme Court referred to the issue. Earlier the Law Commission in its 35ᵗʰ report had recommended the retention of the death penalty. The Supreme Court in Bachan Singh v. Union of India upheld the constitutional validity of the death penalty but restricted it only to the rarest cases. Taking into consideration the changes in the social, economic and cultural contexts of the county since its 35threport with the realization that the death penalty is a sensitive issue the commission decided to take an extensive study. It was held by the commission that the penological goals of deterrence are no more served by the death penalty and that it failed to achieve penological goals. The rehabilitative and restorative aspect was lost and the uneven application has given rise to the state of uncertainty. It was also held that the exercise of mercy power under article 72 and 161 have failed as the final safeguard against the miscarriage of justice. Some of the problems besetting the system included the outdated source of investigation, poor legal aid, resource lack etc. The commission has also recommended that although there is no valid penological justification for treating terrorism different than other crimes however given the concern raised by the lawmakers that it might affect national security. The commission has recommended making it essential for states to establish effective victim compensation schemes to rehabilitate victims of crime. Witness protection scheme was also made essential to protect the voices of victims so that they are not silenced. Effective investigation and better police reforms were felt as the need of the hour.

Mode of execution of death sentence

At present according to Section 354(5) of the Code of Criminal Procedure 1973 the mode of execution of death sentence is hanging till death. In Bachan Singh v Union of India, the Supreme Court observed that the physical pain and suffering which the execution entails is inhumane and cruel. 'The commission has recommended amending section 354(5) of the CRPC by providing an alternative mode of execution of death sentence by lethal injection until the accused is dead'. The convict shall be heard on the question of the mode of the execution of the death sentence before such discretion is exercised. As of now, there is no provision of the right of appeal against the sentence passed by the Court Martial under the Army Act, 1950 the Navy Act, 1957and the Air force act, 1950. It is also recommended that one of the present modes of execution of death that is by hanging should be replaced by administering lethal injection until the accused is dead. The commission finally recommended that death sentence matters should be heard by a five judge's bench of the Supreme Court.

Conclusion

Live is precious and death is irrevocable and every individual must note to keep in mind that none has the right to take away one's life. Still, harsh punishment is required to keep the potential convicts at bay. To protect the life of one convict the lives of thousands of others cannot be risked. Those who are deserving of death should be executed. But some of the people opine that a criminal need to be punished for the crime he committed but we as a civilization need in the direction of eliminating the offence not the illegal. Whether the death penalty should be abolished or not is still a matter of debate and there is no end to it.

Bibliography

Book

Prof.S.N.Mishra ,Indian Penal Code (Edition2015)

Sites

https://lawcommissionofindia.nic.inhttps://www.scconline.com
https://bbc.com

https://docs.manupatra.in

CHAPTER FOUR

ALL ABOUT MEDIA TRIAL

Author: Sanjana Wason, IV year of B.A.,LL.B.(Hons.) from MDU CPAS Sector 40, Gurugram

INTRODUCTION

In this era of digitisation, where every news is just a click away. The role of media has expanded and so has the scope of media trials.

WHAT IS A MEDIA TRIAL?

Trial by media can be described as the impact of media coverage on a case before or after the verdict in a court of law.

HISTORY OF MEDIA TRIAL

The old days of media trials on the court cases go back to the emergency of the printing press. Roscoe Arbuckle was the first celebrity in the 20th century, who was acquitted by the courts but due to strong media influence, he had to lose his career as well as his reputation. Even the case of O.J Simpson, 1995 and Stephen Downing, 2002 also have witnessed the huge impact of the trial by the media.

DOES MEDIA TRIAL COME UNDER THE FREEDOM OF THE PRESS?

Before coming back to the above question let's discuss "Freedom of Press" first.

Freedom of the Press is an indirect right mentioned under Article 19(1)(a) of the Constitution of India. Even in the Constituent Assembly debates Dr B R Amebedkar, Chairman of the Drafting Committee had cleared that there is no special need of mentioning the freedom of the press, as According to him the press and an individual or citizen were the same. And if we talk about media trials, then the Indian Courts have not declared them unconstitutional.

This freedom allows the media to help people in building opinion on various issues of national interest, however, its excess can be a reason for concern. Even According Article 19(1)(2)o of the Indian Constitution has made it apparent that every right can have reasonable restrictions so, the same can be applied to freedom of speech and expression. But can the privacy of an individual be considered as a ground of reasonable restrictions on freedom of speech and expression? So, the answer is NO. Privacy can not be figured as the ground of reasonable restrictions on freedom of speech and expression. Along with the fact that there is no particular legislation in India that give protection against excessive publicity by the press including media trial.

Not long ago, social activists filed a petition before the High Court of Bombay. Where they claimed the agencies investigating Rajput's Case, death leaked personal information to the media, which was then shared with the general public. Here, the Court directed the Central Government to indicate the extent of state control exercised concerning telecasting news having serious results.

TRIAL BY MEDIA AND MEDIA VICTIMIZATION

After witnessing the increasing impact of media trials on the general public, The PRESS COUNCIL OF INDIA (PCI) norms formulate the regulations for reporting cases and avoiding media trials. It warns journalists not to give excessive publicity to an individual may it be victims, witnesses, suspects and accused such that it amounts to an infringement of privacy.

The disclosure of the identity of witnesses may endanger his life or sometimes even his life or sometimes even his loved ones as they may be forced to change their statement in court by coercion or any other methods. Accordingly, The right of privacy of the suspects or accused is being recognised by the PCI to guard against the trial by media.

Swati Deshpande, a senior assistant editor (law) at The Times of India, Mumbai admitted that"Media reporting often gives the impression that the accused has committed the crime or the media through a particular fact. When in fact, it has fallen to the question or verify the fact by an independent source. The result is the information received from the police is rarely questioned."

The 200th Report of the Law Commission (www.lawcommisionofIndia.nic.in/reports) dealt with the issue of Trial by Media: Free speech V. Fair Trial under Criminal Procedure. Where the reports focused on the prejudicial coverage of crime, accused and suspect and how it impacts the administration of justice. As the report emphasises, the pre-trial stage publication by the media could affect the right of the accused. The media has now considered itself, PUBLIC COURT or JANTA ADALAT where it announces its verdict even before the court final judgment.

It keeps the Golden principles of "Presuption of innocence until proven guilty" and "Guilt beyond reasonable doubt"at stake. (Urvashi Singh, "Trial by Media a threat to the administration of justice"http://www.lexology.com)

Pandit Jawaharlal Nehru, the first prime minister of Independent India said -"I would rather have a completely free press with all the dangers involved in the wrong use of that freedom than a suppression of the regulated press ". But he did not expect that the media would go beyond its limit and ultimately hinder the process of administration of justice.

IMPACT OF MEDIA TRIAL ON JUDICIAL PROCEEDING

Media Trials create a huge impact on court proceedings or sometimes even verdicts as well. As evidence can be questionable after the intervention of the media in the investigation of the case.

The influence of media trials not only creates an image in the minds of the general public but also in the mind of Judges as well. So, it becomes the Judge's duty to not let the blind item published in a certain high profile case, affect the case verdict. And since every individual has a right to a free trial, their prejudice can also be considered as contempt of court.

CONCLUSION

In the end, it can be certainly stated that the Media has a right to present facts and figures regarding the National interest of the public but within reasonable restrictions.

REFERENCE

1. Wikipedia
2.iapp.org
3.lawoctopus.com
4. www.legalserviceIndia.com

www.ingramcontent.com/pod-product-compliance
Lightning Source LLC
Chambersburg PA
CBHW050818160726
48004CB00002B/897